Ramadhan and Eid-ul-Fitr

Written and Illustrated by
Azra Jessa

ISBN 13: 978-1-879402-20-1

Published by:

Tahrike Tarsile Qur'an, Inc.
80-08 51st Avenue, Elmhurst, New York 11373-4141
tel: 718-446-6472 fax: 718-446-4370
e: read@koranusa.org
www.koranusa.org

A Note from the Publisher

We hope that you enjoy reading this book. May this serve to be an inspiration for parents to encourage their children to write stories of their own. Bookstores today have few titles that teach the values and beliefs of Islam catered to the youth. In an effort to create a selection of reading material as such, we are asking for children to write and illustrate books, stories and poems about Islam and send us their work to review. We ask parents, teachers and schools to encourage their students to start reading and writing at a young age; some of the best stories for children are ones written by children. We ask for your support in achieving our goal to ensure there are a variety of books for our future generations.

Tahrike Tarsile Qur'an, Inc.
New York

Dedicated To
The Children of Iraq

This book belongs to:

_____

_____

_____

Hi, my name is Azra. I would like to tell you about
two very special holidays that my family and I celebrate.
The holidays are the month of Ramadhan and the
Day after the month of Ramadhan called Eid-ul-Fitr.

I am a Muslim and we follow the lunar calendar. In the lunar calendar, a new month begins when we see the new moon or the crescent. The lunar calendar has 12 months. The number of days in a lunar calendar month is either 29 or 30.

The month of Ramadhan is the month of fasting. Fasting means that you do not drink or eat during the daytime. My parents wake up early in the morning and have breakfast, and they do not eat or drink all day. They break their fasts when the day is over and the sun sets.

In this month all Muslims fast except children, old people and people who are sick. People who are traveling and women who are pregnant are not supposed to fast either.

This fasting seems pretty difficult, doesn't it? But guess what? I tried to do one fast when I was only four years old. It was a little difficult, especially in the afternoon. I was so hungry! But then I thought of the kids in the world who don't have food and that helped me be patient and strong.

I was able to complete the fast! Since this was my first fast, I got a special treat! My dad took me to the toy store and I was allowed to get any toy I wanted. That really made the fast extra special!

In this month we should be extra kind and good to other people. This is called "fasting of our bodies". Our hands should only do good by helping others, our mouths should only be used to say kind words, and our ears should only listen to good things.

After 29 days of fasting, we look at the sky for the new moon or crescent. This new moon is very important because now the month of Ramadhan will be over and we will have a feast. The feast or celebration after the completion of the month of Ramadhan is called "Eid-ul-Fitr" or "Eid."

On the day of Eid, we wear new clothes and go to Mosque for special prayers. Every family has to first give a special amount of money for poor people called "Fitra." We are allowed to celebrate only after we have taken care of people who are in need.

After prayers, we usually visit our family and friends. My parents usually buy us toys. My grandparents give us money as gifts. We eat lots of goodies on the day of Eid and have a special family dinner.

The month of Ramadhan teaches us to control our desires and be kind to others. When we celebrate Eid, we are happy that we have tried to be good and we promise to continue being good for the rest of the year!

EID MUBARAK!

(our way of saying Happy Eid!)

I hope you have enjoyed learning about my special Holidays!

hope

love

dream   play   learn

Child Aid International is an organization that is making a difference in the lives of Iraqi orphans. It is a not-for-profit organization that strives to address the basic needs of orphaned children in Iraq by providing them with hope, inspiration and support to develop into healthy, caring, and confident individuals.

The war in Iraq has devastated thousands of lives - families have been destroyed, homes have been lost, and countless children have been orphaned. With generous donor support, Child Aid International sponsors impoverished orphaned children in Iraq. Sponsorship covers the cost of healthcare, food, clothing, and education for an orphaned child.

Child Aid International has also initiated various special projects to help orphaned Iraqi children such as its holiday gift program (successfully implemented in both 2005 and 2006), and its shipment of a container of essential medical supplies and clothing to Iraq in August, 2006.

Child Aid International strives to help orphaned children in Iraq regardless of gender, race, ethnicity or faith. After all, every child deserves to have its dream fulfilled.

For more information please visit www.childaidinternational.org

child aid
INTERNATIONAL